Original title:
Field of Free Verse

Copyright © 2025 Creative Arts Management OÜ
All rights reserved.

Author: Elias Marchant
ISBN HARDBACK: 978-1-80566-635-6
ISBN PAPERBACK: 978-1-80566-920-3

Starlit Journeys of Expression

Under the sky, we take a leap,
With scribbles and doodles, not meant to keep.
A dance on paper, oh what a sight,
Words turn to giggles, under the starlight.

Puns fly like fireflies, buzzing around,
In this playful chaos, laughter is found.
A sonnet sings funny, a haiku trips too,
Each line brings a smile, just like brand-new glue.

The Harmony of Unrestricted Voices

Voices collide in a joyous spree,
A chorus of nonsense, just let it be.
Each note a chuckle, each word a jest,
Together we whistle, it's simply the best.

Outrageous tales leap off the page,
Characters waltz in a playful rage.
With every rhyme, the silliness grows,
A symphony spun from the wildest prose.

Reflections on Untamed Pages

Pages flip wildly, as thoughts take flight,
In this wacky wonder, things feel just right.
A mirror that giggles, a canvas so sly,
Reflecting our quirks, like clouds in the sky.

Words wiggle and jiggle, like jelly on toast,
We celebrate nonsense and humor the most.
Each sentence a laugh, each paragraph plays,
In this quirky library, we spend our days.

Waves of Unbound Creativity

Riding the ripples of ideas so bright,
Each splash is a chuckle, a burst of delight.
We surf through the verses, catching the fun,
With humor our paddle, we'll never be done.

A sea of expressions, all wild and free,
In this ocean of laughter, just you and me.
With every new wave, we rise and we fall,
In this quirky adventure, we're having a ball.

The Unraveling of Structured Silence

In a world where rules are bent,
The silence starts to hum and vent.
Penguins in tuxedos dance a jig,
While cats debate the plight of a twig.

Mice throw parties, cheese galore,
As squirrels plan heists—what's next in store?
The birds critique the fashion of trees,
With every breeze, they flit with ease.

Laughter leaks from every crack,
As rabbits argue, 'Who's on track?'
Snails race slowly, a true delight,
And fireflies flash through the night.

So let's embrace this rumpled cheer,
And giggle loudly, let's have no fear.
In chaos, joy finds its place,
As structured silence picks up the pace.

The Breath of Sprawled Narratives

Words tumble out like socks on a line,
Each tale a mix of pickle and brine.
Turtles perform acrobatic flips,
While ants scribble stories on potato chips.

Butterflies boast of kingdoms they've seen,
While frogs argue over what's truly green.
The wise old owl scratches his head,
Saying, 'Try tales on a loaf of bread.'

Llamas recite poems under the sun,
While goldfish debate who's having the fun.
A sandwich confesses it's feeling quite bland,
Then suddenly dreams of a food-themed band.

When narratives stretch from here to the moon,
Laughter erupts like a jubilant tune.
Let's join the mélange of stories anew,
And embrace the wild with a chuckle or two.

Reflections on the Boundless Path

There's a path made of jellybeans, quite odd,
Where unicorns prance and give a nod.
The flowers gossip in giggly tones,
While hedgehogs plan to join the drones.

Pebbles roll like they're in a race,
As frogs play tag with an errant lace.
Every step's a new choreography,
In a place where reality's a fun parody.

Clouds fluff up like cotton candy dreams,
As squirrels devise their grander schemes.
Wandering geese in top hats march by,
Whilst a snail comments on fashion with a sigh.

So stroll down this path, embrace the absurd,
With laughter and play, let joy be stirred.
In the wild of whimsy, life's bright and vast,
Join in the fun, and let's have a blast!

The Tides of Unfettered Words

Words tumble like crayons,
Rolling off the table,
Chasing after a cat,
Who declares it's fable.

Puns swim in the ocean,
Dancing with the waves,
A rubber duck parade,
In tiny poetic caves.

Rhyme schemes play hopscotch,
Jumping here and there,
While laughter's the anchor,
Tied without a care.

Metaphors are beach balls,
Bouncing overhead,
Chasing after sunlight,
While silliness is fed.

Seeds of Improv in the Air

A juggling act of jest,
With banana peels in tow,
Sprouting wild ideas,
As if they grow and glow.

A hiccup in the laughter,
A slip upon a pun,
Each line a wild sprout,
In the orchard of the fun.

Silly thoughts take to flight,
Like kites upon the breeze,
Each giggle a new flight,
Spreading joy with ease.

Ideas bloom like daisies,
In mismatched socks they play,
Twisting into laughter,
In a most absurd way.

Mapping the Poetry of the Unseen

Invisible ink scribbles,
Across an empty page,
A cartographer of laughter,
Who draws without a cage.

Doodles dance like shadows,
Waltzing in the night,
Each stroke a little secret,
In the absence of the light.

Mapping out the giggles,
With crayons made of cheer,
Finding paths to silliness,
For all the world to hear.

The compass spins in circles,
Guiding where we roam,
As we explore tomorrow,
In poetry, we're home.

The Flow of Limitless Expression

In the rivers of my mind,
Words float like rubber ducks,
Paddling through the giggles,
With hugs and silly chuckles.

Expression swims like fish,
With fins of rainbow hues,
Every splash a giggle,
In the sea of maybe blues.

A filter made of laughter,
Catching poems as they fly,
Each line a wave of nonsense,
Bubbling toward the sky.

Limitless is the current,
That twists around the day,
Where humor finds a rhythm,
In a most delightful way.

The Meadow of Poetic Wanderings

In a place where rhymes take flight,
The words are dancing, feeling light.
A squirrel's joke makes poets grin,
   As daisies giggle in the wind.

Thoughts collide like bees in bloom,
Rabbits sketch beneath the gloom.
The sun spills laughter, bright and bold,
While ants tell tales of days of old.

Each stanza skips, a playful breeze,
Where dandelions float with ease.
In free-form frolic, rhymes collide,
   In every corner, joy does hide.

So come, my friends, embrace the cheer,
Join the merry dance, have no fear.
In this meadow, fun's the goal,
Wordplay's magic ignites the soul.

Gravity of Unwritten Thoughts

Bouncing ideas like a bouncy ball,
Dropping puns, they rise for all.
Thoughts that tumble, twist and spin,
In absent lines, the fun begins.

A paper airplane flops and twirls,
While laughter curls like frothy swirls.
Gravity pulls, but humor soars,
As we scribble out poetic chores.

Words defy the limits set,
In this chaotic fine duet.
A rubber chicken in each verse,
Bouncing like a playful curse.

In every blank, a joke awaits,
The comedy, it fluctuates.
Embrace absurdity, take your chance,
Let all your thoughts wildly dance.

Dance of the Unstructured Muse

The muse wears sneakers, big and bright,
Jumps rope with shadows in the night.
Words trip over their mismatched shoes,
As laughter echoes, gleeful blues.

She twirls through clouds of cotton candy,
Sprinkling joy; it's sweet and dandy.
With scribbles on a neon page,
A dance of freedom, bold and sage.

Her rhythm's quirky, steps askew,
She pirouettes on a pen of blue.
Each line's a giggle, stitched with glee,
As we all join her jubilee.

With every jive, the chaos sways,
In this whirl of whimsical displays.
Embrace the absurd, let laughter shake,
In this joyful dance where dreams awake.

Verses in the Wilderness

In the woods, where words run wild,
The trees, they whisper, giggle, and smiled.
A bear recites on a rock so grand,
While owls hoot jokes only they understand.

Squirrels recite rhymes with flair,
As wind carries chuckles through the air.
Each line a twig, each laugh a leaf,
Nature's comedy, beyond belief.

In tangled lines, the fun begins,
As frogs croak out their playful sins.
Mushrooms chat in puns galore,
As laughter blooms at the forest floor.

So come, explore this quirky place,
Where words embrace, and rhymes embrace.
In the wilderness where fun abounds,
Let laughter be the only sound.

The Pulse of Uncharted Thoughts

In the garden where ideas sprout,
A chicken dances, laughing out loud.
It claims it's clever, a thinking bird,
While kangaroos manage to spread the word.

A cat wears glasses, reads a book,
With wisdom that stuns—just take a look.
It ponders life, but then it snores,
Dreaming of fish and open doors.

A snail speeds past, in a rush for tea,
While a turtle shouts, "Just wait for me!"
They debate on weather, clouds, and sun,
Who knew the great world had such fun?

So gather 'round in this quirky place,
Where oddball thoughts come out to race.
It's laughter and joy, a whimsical spree,
In the land of nonsense, we all agree!

Whims of the Infinite

The moon wears a hat made of cheese,
While stars giggle softly in the breeze.
A comet dressed bright, with sequins galore,
Invites the planets for an interstellar tour.

The sun does a jig, shines a goofy grin,
As laughter echoes through the solar din.
Mercury grumps, says, "I'm burning up!"
While Venus spills tea from a fancy cup.

Jupiter's storms swirl with laughter and cheer,
It tells silly tales that all want to hear.
Saturn sports rings that jingle around,
Creating a rhythm that's joyfully sound.

In this cosmic dance, all come alive,
With quirks and jests, they happily thrive.
It's a universe of humor, vast and bright,
Where every oddity is pure delight!

Crossover of Boundless Imagination

A pencil dreams of being a sword,
In a duel with paper, it's never bored.
Erasers cheer and throw confetti high,
As paperclips fly and reach for the sky.

A scribble hops, doing a jig,
While rulers stretch, they're feeling big.
Glue sticks gossip about crafty schemes,
Creating new worlds from wild, wacky dreams.

A crayon spins tales in colors so bold,
Of dragons and knights and treasures untold.
With laughter it colors, it giggles and sings,
For in this realm, anything can have wings!

So join this wild, imaginative ride,
Where thoughts and dreams ignite our pride.
With humor and flair, let's turn the page,
And celebrate whimsy at every stage!

The Swell of Unrestricted Words

Words tumble out like a playful stream,
A chatterbox dancing, living the dream.
They trip over giggles, float in the air,
While sentences twirl, without a care.

Adjectives wiggle, verbs leap with glee,
While nouns play tag, as happy as can be.
Exclamations burst with excitement and fun,
While whispers sneak in, trying to run.

Puns stretch their limbs, ready to joke,
As metaphors puff and happily poke.
In this wacky world where language is king,
Each silly phrase makes the heart want to sing.

So let's gather 'round and share our delight,
In a playground of words, where all is light.
With laughter and whimsy, let's take a stand,
For in this embrace, we'll all understand!

Whispers of Untamed Words

In the garden of jest, where giggles bloom,
Puns dance lightly, dispelling the gloom.
A wordsmith's playground, where laughter's the goal,
Each line a tickle, each stanza a stroll.

The cats wear hats, and the dogs sing tunes,
As cookies converse with the twinkling moons.
Silly hats flurry like butterflies bright,
Here humor reigns, from morning till night.

Banana peels slip in a rhythm divine,
Jokes tumble freely like bubbles in wine.
Amidst fleeting phrases, the punchlines are spry,
Otters recite while the frogs leap high.

So come take a dip in this pool of bright cheer,
Where nonsense is nectar, and laughter draws near.
With a wink and a wiggle, let's turn up the fun,
In this whimsical realm, where words never shun.

Elysium of Expression

In a land where cacti wear spectacles wide,
And lilies debate with pride on the side.
The daisies cartwheel, the roses debate,
While bees throw confetti at a snail's first date.

Prancing in puddles, the toads share a grin,
As the hedgehogs argue who's winning the spin.
With wobbly words and a jiggle of tone,
Each sentence is served on a laughter-filled cone.

The squirrels recite with a twirl and a flip,
While the sunbeams join in on this comical trip.
A toast with the blossoms to jesters out loud,
For the humor unchained is the boldest of crowds.

So let's pen a tale where nonsense is king,
Where giggles and chuckles are always in swing.
Through this maze of laughter, we'll skip and we'll soar,
In this joyous abode, where the wise never bore.

Canvas of the Unchained

On this canvas of giggles, the colors run wild,
With crayons of whimsy, let every heart smile.
The rainbows play hide and seek with the clouds,
As elephants waltz in their fanciest shrouds.

A paintbrush winks, doodles dance in the air,
Cucumbers gossip, with attitude rare.
The brushes chat softly, while canvases sigh,
And giraffes argue who's taller, oh my!

Framed in a jest, where the parodies glide,
They mix in the colors, let laughter abide.
A tickle of paint on a bachelor heart,
Where every spilled ink holds a humorous art.

So dip in your palette, let merriment flow,
In this madness of talent, where giggles do grow.
We'll sketch out the jokes and sculpt out the cheer,
In this unshackled space, let creativity steer.

Verses in the Wind

As verses take flight, like kites in the breeze,
The whispers of laughter slip through the trees.
With ticklish thoughts trailing behind like a kite,
Each phrase that we write is a spark of delight.

The clouds share their secrets, the sun plays around,
While squirrels compose in a musical sound.
Mirth lives in the rustle, the giggles swirl free,
In a verse-flying journey, come fly along, see!

The wind carries stories, like feathers in flight,
Tickling our senses, all day and all night.
A chorus of chatter, that tickles the ear,
With each taunting breeze, the punchlines draw near.

So let's sail on the whimsy, in laughter we'll sail,
With verses aloft, we will never grow stale.
Join this breezy parade, let your spirit unwind,
In the whirlwind of humor, let joy be our bind.

Sketches in an Open Sky

In the clouds, I drew a cat,
But it rained and fell splat.
Birds perched, giving me a nod,
Thinking my art is quite odd.

A plane zoomed by, left a trail,
I waved and choked on a pail.
A unicorn formed, just for fun,
Until the sun said, "I'm done!"

The sky turned pink, with tints of blue,
Kites danced like they were new.
Laughter bounced from ear to ear,
As clouds played peek-a-boo here.

In this vast and quirky dome,
Even farts can find a home.
So let your giggles roam wild,
For life's a canvas, like a child.

Celebration of the Unfenced Spirit

A chicken crossed the road, they say,
Chasing freedom, not full pay.
It strutted wide with feathery flair,
Bumped into a goat who didn't care.

Dancing in a field of misplaced socks,
The cows party and throw rocks.
They moo like they've lost their minds,
Chasing butterflies and skipping lines.

The sunbeams dance, oh what a sight,
Stars in the day, what a delight!
We wear our hats twisted like so,
Who knew goats and chickens stole the show?

Outside the paddock, there's no fence,
Just laughter, joy, a bit of suspense.
Let's toast to a life that's sweet and free,
Where even ants have their own jamboree!

Mapping the Terrain of Thought

In a maze of mismatched shoes,
I find the paths I didn't choose.
Each thought a flickering firefly,
 Buzzing 'round like a weird pie.

My brain's a map, all dotted lines,
With signals crossed like tangled twines.
 A GPS that leads to snacks,
 Not wisdom, but tasty hacks.

Over hills of wonky dreams,
I stumble in my mind's extremes.
Twirl and trip, my compass spins,
 Is that laughter? Oh, it begins!

In a land where socks can talk,
And broccoli plays hopscotch in chalk,
Let's scribble wildly, come what may,
For thoughts are silly in their own way.

A Symphony Without Borders

In a world where spoons can sing,
And rubber ducks play the bling,
An orchestra of giggles reigns,
As a giraffe leaps like it's a game.

Piano keys like jelly beans,
Tickle toes of laughing queens.
While fish in tuxedos swim around,
To the rhythm of splashes, oh what a sound!

A cat on drums, with furry might,
Cymbals crash, what a delight!
Harmony of quirks in every note,
As giggling snails take up the quote.

So here's a toast to joyful noise,
In this merry land with laughing toys.
They say it's chaos and can't conform,
But darling, it's a raucous storm!

The Passage of Fluid Lines

In a land where squiggles roam,
Noodles dance and poets comb.
Chasing rhymes that flutter away,
Like loose socks in a dryer's play.

Pencils rolling, slipping down,
Writing jokes in a scribbled frown.
Words jump high and then they flop,
As lines of humor never stop.

A comma trips, a period sings,
Metaphors wear bright-colored things.
With laughter echoing from the pen,
It seems the stanza likes to bend.

Resonance of the Unconfined

In a world where verses shout,
Puns are kings, and doubts are out.
Syllables soar on a trampoline,
While similes wear polka-dot sheen.

There's a grand parade of playful trees,
Juggling words like bees in the breeze.
Each punchline lands with a silly thud,
As metaphors wander in a mud.

Rhyme schemes sip on fizzy drinks,
As syntax giggles, and logic stinks.
With each new twist, a laugh unfolds,
Where every verse is purest gold.

Whispers of Untamed Stanzas

Once there was a line so bold,
It told a tale that never grew old.
It teetered on the edge of rhyme,
Mother Goose would envy its time.

While joking with a cheeky pun,
The stanza said, "Let's have some fun!"
With ticklish syllables on parade,
They teased the world, unafraid.

Each word a giggle, each pause a wink,
Rhythms dance while critics sink.
In this land, nonsense is king,
Where laughter is the truest thing.

Unchained Lines of the Heart

Lines that prance without a care,
Mischievous words that float in air.
A heart that beats to a bouncy tune,
Like silly cats beneath the moon.

When laughter spills on pages bright,
Each couplet plays with sheer delight.
Sentences chase, words giggle and tease,
Poking fun at grammatical thieves.

With metaphors that dance in socks,
And rhythm wrapped in paradox.
Join the fun, abandon strife,
For laughter is the key to life.

Harmonies of the Heart

In a world where ducks wear hats,
They waddle by, and nothing bats.
A rabbit sings a slightly off key,
And the sun giggles behind a tree.

The flowers dance, they twist and yell,
Spreading joy, like a funny spell.
A butterfly spins, then does a dive,
Saying, "Hey folks, I'm really alive!"

With cats in ties and dogs in crowns,
The laughter blankets all the towns.
Every tune a silly twist,
In a symphony no one can resist.

So join the fun, the jubilant art,
Where nonsense lives, and joy takes part.
For every beat is just a spark,
Of shimmering jokes that hit the mark.

The Lyrical Meadow

In a meadow where the cows all clown,
With polka dots and silly gowns.
The daisies gossip as they sway,
Telling secrets in a breezy way.

Grasshoppers host a rather grand ball,
While crickets chuckle, the best of all.
A squirrel tries to juggle grapes,
And the trees lean in, stifling the gapes.

With bees reciting absurd old poems,
Even the pond plays along with its loams.
A frog in glasses writes down the laughs,
In a journal filled with silly drafts.

So come and see this whimsical sight,
Where every moment feels just right.
Let giggles bloom under the bright sun,
In this place, where silliness runs!

Unscripted Journeys

A snail packed up for a trip today,
With a tiny suitcase, hip-hip-hooray!
He slipped and slid, a sticky sight,
Claiming, "Traveling's a real delight!"

The tortoise joins with a map so grand,
But in the mud, he can barely stand.
He points left, then he points right,
And protests, "This can't be quite right!"

The birds above laugh and coo,
At how the journey's rarely true.
They fly zigzag, the stars align,
Singing, "Navigating is just divine!"

With each wrong turn, they call it fun,
Every misstep adds to the run.
Adventures bloom like daisies bright,
In a world where wrongs make it right.

Rhythm of the Unbounded

A raccoon strums on a bass guitar,
While a goose hums along from afar.
The rhythm shakes the leaves above,
Creating beats that we all love.

The ants parade with fancy hats,
Grooving along like acrobats.
Their tiny feet tap-dance in glee,
Proclaiming, "Dance harder, just be free!"

The moon winks down with a silver grin,
As nightfall comes, let the fun begin!
With twinkling stars that sway and dive,
This joyous pulse makes us alive.

So shake your tail and swirl around,
In this moment, let laughter resound.
For every heartbeat sings a tune,
Under the gazing, giggling moon.

Gypsy Lines of Emotion

In the circus of my brain, they dance,
Clowns in thought, they twist and prance.
Juggling dreams, they drop a few,
Spinning tales like morning dew.

A cat in boots begins to sing,
While socks unite to form a ring.
They laugh at life, they twist their fate,
In mismatched hats, they celebrate.

A rubber chicken takes a stroll,
With crazy thoughts that take a toll.
But who says logic's got to win?
When silly thoughts feel like a sin?

So here we are, a silly crew,
With giggles bursting like the dew.
The magic lies in every rhyme,
Where nonsense twists and bends with time.

Dialogues of Daring Ideas

Two zebras chat on grassy bliss,
One says, 'Life's a crazy kiss!'
The other thinks it's all a ruse,
'You can't wear stripes without a bruise!'

A dodo bird flies high in dreams,
Sipping tea from flowery streams.
Whenever doubts begin to creep,
They giggle, thinking sleep's for sheep.

Whispers of ideas spin like tops,
A snail claims he can win the hops.
The turtles chime, 'We take our time!'
While plotting schemes that feel sublime.

And here we stand, in doodle-space,
With wobbly thoughts that we embrace.
Let's ride the wave of laughter's flight,
And dance amidst the starry night.

Refrain of the Unrestricted

A penguin in a tutu twirls,
While jellybeans do cartwheel swirls.
The sun wears shades and takes a dive,
In this odd world, we start to jive.

A squirrel recites Shakespeare with pride,
As acorns bounce from side to side.
Oh, the drama of nutty bliss,
Can sweetness really be amiss?

Marshmallow clouds fluff up the sky,
While gummy bears begin to fly.
They plot world peace with sticky hands,
In this candy land, fun never stands.

So listen close, oh hearts so light,
Where whimsy reigns in pure delight.
For in this realm of laughter's club,
We find our joy in every snub.

The Untethered Narrative

Once a frog wore shoes too tight,
He hopped around with all his might.
He tripped on flies, a real hoot,
And ended up in quite a suit.

A toaster dreams of flying high,
While burning bread, it starts to cry.
'I'm meant for more than just the toasts!'
It wishes hard on morning ghosts.

A dancing broom sweeps up the mess,
It says, 'Why not? I must confess!
I long to dance, to spin and play,
Each sweep is just a wacky ballet!'

So laugh with me, oh kindred soul,
In tales of whim where we feel whole.
For life, dear heart, is wild and free,
A narrative with glee, you'll see!

Glimmers of Wild Creativity

In a land where ideas sprout,
Ideas dance like cows about.
Stripes and polka dots join in,
As laughter bursts from each whim.

Toasters sing while cats wear hats,
Dancing gophers and fancy spats.
We juggle thoughts with silly flair,
And twirl in socks, without a care.

Imagination's doors swing wide,
No need for maps, we just glide.
We ride on worms that giggle too,
In this place where dreams come true.

With crayons in our cereal bowls,
And jellybeans that speak in scrolls.
The sun wears shades, the clouds wear ties,
In our world of joyful surprise.

Echoes of Verses Afloat

Bubbles burst with rhymes and glee,
A fish sings opera from the sea.
Trees play chess with the rising moon,
While squirrels toss acorns in tune.

Bananas slip on sandy shores,
Cartwheeling crabs request encores.
The ocean whispers silly jokes,
As jellyfish perform with folks.

Seagulls wear sunglasses so bright,
And squawk about the latest flight.
Pineapples laugh beneath a tree,
Inviting all to join their spree.

This watery carnival does not fade,
As giggles echo, unafraid.
We paddle in a sea of cheer,
In this place where joy is near.

The Rhythm of Unharnessed Souls

Kites take flight like thoughts unchained,
With strings that break when fun is gained.
Rhythms bounce on trampoline skies,
While marshmallow clouds do acrobatics that surprise.

We chase our shadows, paint them bright,
In a dance-off with the stars tonight.
The moon taps toes, the sun does spins,
And laughter lifts us on silly wins.

Light bulbs shatter with giggles loud,
As we embrace the quirky crowd.
With socks mismatched on little feet,
Each step becomes an outrageous beat.

Unharnessed joy fills the air,
And silly hats are everywhere.
We leap and twirl with hearts so light,
In this tune of pure delight.

Patterns in the Unplowed Dirt

Worms leave trails that twist and turn,
While daisies shout, "We'd like a burn!"
Patting dirt with silly hands,
Crafting castles made of sands.

Crickets chirp a funky song,
While frogs harmonize along.
The wind whispers jokes to the patch,
As mud pies rise, not a scratch!

Ants parade in a wobbly line,
Wearing tiny hats that shine.
Butterflies tease the buzzing bees,
In a wild race through the trees.

With funny shapes in earthy hue,
We sculpt our dreams anew.
In this patch of sprightly fun,
We find our laughter, everyone.

Echoes in the Open Air

Loud laughter floats, the breeze displays,
Chasing pigeons in clumsy ballet.
Silly hats dance on heads like clowns,
Every giggle echoes, spreading the sounds.

A snail slides by, with pace so grand,
While kids play tag, they can't quite stand.
The flowers nod, they join the cheer,
As bees buzz in, insisting they're near.

Umbrellas turn, as clouds start to spill,
Rain dances down, can't hold the thrill.
A puddle forms, it's now a pool,
Splashing around, how wild and cool!

Come join the fun, leave worries aside,
In this open space, it's joy we confide.
With every laugh, create a new tale,
In the open air, we'll never derail.

Fragmented Harmonies of the Heart

A cat sings opera, what a strange sight,
While dogs take notes; it's quite a delight.
Chairs start to dance; they wiggle and sway,
In this odd concert, who'll lead the way?

A frog plays the tambourine, so loud,
While crickets chirp, stirring up the crowd.
Butterflies leap, they're part of the band,
As nature claps with a magical hand.

Bananas slide in a comedic review,
While ants in tuxedos coordinate too.
With each silly note, the heart skips and bounds,
In this joyous mess, true bliss abounds.

So gather around, let spirits ascend,
In this playful symphony, let laughter blend.
With every weird sound, embrace the absurd,
In the harmony of chaos, joy is assured.

Sparks of Unfenced Creativity

A canvas flipped, colors fly high,
With brushes that giggle, oh my, oh my!
Splashes of orange, a dab of green,
These strokes of madness all form a scene.

Crayons march, they're ready to play,
Creating rainbows in a most goofy way.
A squiggle here, a wibble there,
Art is a party; let's color the air!

Giraffes wear glasses, so chic and wise,
While zebras skateboard, to everyone's surprise.
Doodles sprout legs and run to the front,
In this creative chaos, there's always a stunt.

So unleash those brushes, don't hold them back,
In this silly journey, let's be off track.
With every wild stroke, let laughter ignite,
In this vibrant mess, creativity takes flight.

Lost in the Wildness of Expression

In the wild a raccoon recites a sonnet,
While squirrels in top hats all race to be honest.
Amidst the tall grass, tigers rehearse,
Their dramatic tales, oh how they converse!

A chicken in high heels struts down the lane,
Chasing a fox, who's gone slightly insane.
They tap dance together, a most curious pair,
Under the big skies, with humor to spare.

The sun starts to giggle, casting its light,
While shadows join in, oh what a sight!
A whispering wind tells jokes from the dome,
In nature's wild world, we all feel at home.

So join in the frolic, let your heart race,
With every wild moment, find your own space.
In the wildness of thought, let laughter explode,
For the joy of expression is a wondrous road.

Chasing Shadows of Spontaneity

In the garden, squirrels dance,
Wearing hats of sheer mischance.
I trip on grass that's full of glee,
And laugh as they play tricks on me.

A cat throws shade, a feather flies,
While butterflies wear tiny ties.
I chase my thoughts like bubbles blown,
Each one pops, a silly moan.

Laughter bubbles from the streams,
Tangled up in silly dreams.
A toad croaks jokes, the sun complies,
Nature's jesters, oh what a surprise!

With every step, a giggle shared,
The world unruly, yet unscared.
Chasing shadows, wild and free,
A merry ring of comedy.

Surfaces Where Light Collides

Reflections swirl in playful rays,
A fish remarks on sunny days.
The sky's a canvas, splashed with cheer,
While clouds wear coats of smoke and beer.

A bee in striped pajamas hums,
Bouncing 'round as laughter thrums.
Ice cream drips on someone's nose,
That's where the sweetest chaos grows!

Mirrors giggle at the sight,
Of butterflies dancing, oh so bright.
Every glimmer feels like fun,
When sunlight nudges everyone!

We skip along the shimmering edge,
Hearts in tune, we make a pledge.
To find the joy in every tide,
On surfaces where light collides.

The Drift of Freeform Reflections

Whimsical waves that twist and turn,
A rubber duck gives life a churn.
I ride the laughter on a leaf,
In this realm, there's no belief.

A pickle whispers to a sock,
"What's so funny? Tick-tock, tick-tock!"
As sunlight drips from every branch,
The world's a stage, let's do a dance!

In puddles, jokes are softly spilled,\nWhile daisies giggle, petals thrilled.
Each step we take, a chance to find,
A fit of laughter, joy entwined!

Reflections drift like crazy streams,
In this place, we weave our dreams.
Unfettered thoughts roam wild and free,
In this dance of pure hilarity.

Journeys beyond the Horizon

We set off towards the silly sun,
With polka-dot balloons for fun.
Maps drawn in crayon, full of flair,
   Guiding us to everywhere!

Adventures wait on every street,
Bouncing clowns and talking feet.
A journey takes on quirky phrases,
Where each twist leads to smiling gazes.

The breeze hums tunes of yesteryear,
   As poppy flowers lend an ear.
Chasing dreams as we explore,
   A carnival of laughs galore!

Across the bridge of whimsy's lane,
We chase the echo of our gain.
In every moment, joy takes flight,
Journeys beyond, a pure delight!

Echoes of a Dreamer's Mind

In my head, cats wear hats,
Chasing dreams on roller skates.
Clouds play chess with the sun,
While I sip on fizzy fates.

Toasters toast their favorite bread,
But only when I sing aloud.
Jellybeans dance in my shoes,
Making my missteps proud.

A llama leaps with grace and flair,
Spinning wheelies on a dime.
Each thought's a quirky little flare,
Tickling my mind like a mime.

With giggles bouncing off the walls,
Reality's a jester bright.
In this circus of the soul,
Every shadow bursts with light.

Boundless Terrain of Thought

Here's a world where fish can fly,
And squirrels steal the moon's embrace.
A snail races with a pie,
As time drips down with sweet grace.

Rabbits wear polka-dot suits,
Debating art and classic lore.
While wise old owls play their flutes,
And hoot about the supermarket's store.

A cactus starts a dance-off spree,
With tumbleweeds as its crew.
My brain's a circus, can't you see?
With acrobats that break right through.

Every thought's a bouncy ball,
That lands with laughter in my mind.
Chasing them feels like a crawl,
Yet every moment's one of a kind.

The Symphony of Solitude

In silence, a tap-dancing frog,
Composes tunes on lily pads.
Balloons float by, whispering fog,
As dreams take on their jester's fads.

A cactus sings the blues at night,
With crickets tapping out the beat.
Moonlight twirls in sheer delight,
While ants run off with a treat.

My thoughts play chess, with wild flair,
Each piece a giggle, bold and bright.
The echoes of this quiet air,
Proclaim solitude's happy light.

In corners where my whimsy roams,
Jokes tumble like leaves from a tree.
Here, I find no need for homes,
Just a jester's song, wild and free.

No Borders in the Breeze

Running barefoot through my dreams,
A breeze whispers 'Catch the fun!'
Kites adorned like laughing schemes,
Chase the daisies, one by one.

Jellyfish on bicycles glide,
Waving hello to fish in ties.
The sun crashes a dance party wide,
As shadows twirl and do laps in the skies.

No walls can hold these bursts of cheer,
With smiles that bounce upon the track.
Clouds join in without a fear,
Painting laughter, no turning back.

As I roll in this wild spree,
Every gust brings forth a grin.
No borders in the breeze, you see,
Just joy that dances from within.

Palette of the Poet's Soul

Colors swirl in my mind's eye,
A purple cat wearing a tie.
I dip my brush in dreams so bold,
Painted words that never grow old.

Limericks dance on a canvas bright,
With rhymes that take flight at night.
A waltz of whimsy and jest,
Tickling thoughts, a humorous quest.

Each hue speaks in a giggle and grin,
A splash of laughter, let's begin.
With silly shapes and glorious mess,
The poet's soul in vibrant dress.

Grab your palette, come along,
Let's scribble verses, sing a song.
In this playhouse of playful mind,
Joy in creation, laughter defined.

Unleashing the Inmost Voice

Whispers hidden in cobwebs of thought,
Voices that giggle, but rarely are caught.
I chase them around like a cat on the prowl,
But all I get back is a raucous howl.

A parrot perched on my shoulder squawks,
"Write me a poem!" and loudly talks.
With every word, it flaps its wings,
Spilling my secrets, oh, the joy it brings!

Between the lines come the chuckles and snorts,
Riding the waves of my silly retorts.
Each phrase a spark, igniting the night,
My inmost voice finally taking flight.

In laughter, we find a freedom that glows,
Catch this wild wind, see how it flows.
With every howl and chirp in my ear,
I unleash my heart and let go of fear.

Chasing the Fleeting Phrase

With a magnifying glass, I hunt for the muse,
A slippery thought in colorful shoes.
It dashes and darts, like a mouse in a maze,
Eluding my grasp, that clever phrase!

I trip on the words, they giggle and tease,
"Catch me if you can!" they say with ease.
Across the page, they wiggle and swirl,
In a wacky, wild, grammatical whirl.

A stanza jumps up, does a cartwheel in glee,
While metaphors march in a jubilant spree.
I laugh and I stumble, writing this chase,
Each corner turned reveals a new place.

But just when I think I've mounted the prize,
My clever phrase slips past my eyes.
With a wink, it vanishes, what a fun race,
Chasing these musings through time and space!

Starlit Pathways of Prose

Under the stars, my ideas stroll,
Wobbling like jelly, out of control.
Puns and jests float around like balloons,
Tickling the night with tune-filled tunes.

Each sentence struts with a jaunty flair,
Like a penguin in tux, debonair.
They bump into commas, laugh at the frowns,
In this wordy circus, no one wears crowns.

I follow the trail of the squeaky clean verse,
Where humor rolls out like a playful curse.
With whimsy entwined and laughter in tow,
These starlit pathways always aglow.

So come take a stroll, let's giggle and play,
In this prose-party where wordsmiths sway.
We'll dance with ideas, make merriment rare,
In the smiling shadows, joy hangs in the air.

Blossoms of Unbridled Expression

In a garden where giggles bloom,
Petals dance in a comical room.
Butterflies laugh at the blooms' winks,
While daisies gossip and plot with the drinks.

Bumblebees buzz with a silly tune,
Critters join in, under the bright moon.
Each flower prances with joy so loud,
Creating a bouquet that makes you proud.

The sun tickles buds, they burst into cheer,
Each whiff is a laugh, can you hear?
A tulip made jokes of its floppy hat,
Even roses chortle, imagine that!

Amidst the laughter, blooms take a chance,
With petals pirouetting, they prance.
Nature's humor, let it unfold,
Weave smiles in colors so bold.

Traces of an Uncharted Mind

Wanders of thought in a jumbled spree,
Ideas pop like popcorn, wild and free.
A notion once shy, leaps on the page,
With antics so silly, it steals the stage.

Sketches of dreams with crayons in hand,
Draw droll scenarios that are just grand.
Fish wear sunglasses, cats ride in cars,
With laughter that echoes to the nearest stars.

Surrealism's jester, absurd and spry,
Doodles that giggle, oh my, oh my!
Thoughts crisscross like spaghetti untold,
Each noodle a laugh, in the playful fold.

Lost in the quirk of a whimsical ride,
Logic takes off, it's just not applied.
With scribbles and smirks, all worries unwind,
These traces of thought, so delightfully blind.

The Currents of Improvised Dreams

Floating on currents, dreams take a leap,
Splashing with colors, into giggles they seep.
Clouds in a row find mischief to make,
As raindrops play tag, oh what a wake!

A river of laughter flows wild and bright,
Whirling with thoughts in a dance of delight.
Each wave a chuckle, each ripple a grin,
The waters of whimsy invite you to swim.

Bubbles float up, with secrets in tow,
Jests of the mind in the ebb and the flow.
Anchors of seriousness tossed out to sea,
In waves of amusement, we're totally free.

These currents of jest, they carry us far,
To shores where we find, we're all a bit bizarre.
With each splash of joy, we weave and we dream,
In this spirited stream, we all share the gleam.

Wildflowers of Spontaneous Thought

In the meadow of mind, wildflowers sprout,
Whirling in colors, they twist and they shout.
Petals unfurl with a pop and a zing,
Nature's own jester, on whimsy they cling.

Sunflowers giggle at shadows that hide,
While tulips burst forth, in laughter they bide.
Dandelions puff with a chuckle so bright,
As wishes take flight like a kite at first light.

Butterflies flutter, in patterns so free,
Each flap a laugh, oh, what joy to see!
Nature's punchline in every green blade,
Sowing hilarity, in sunshine displayed.

As weeds weave in, with their unruly charm,
They join the bouquet, creating the balm.
In this riot of joy, we plant every thought,
A patchwork of humor that life never bought.

The Echoing Silence

In the quiet park, a duck does quack,
While a squirrel dances, with a sneaky snack.
The trees hold secrets, the grass holds glee,
As I ponder life, and sip my sweet tea.

A spider spins stories, in webs all around,
Hoping a fly would tumble down, bound.
The wind whispers jokes, but I can't catch one,
So I laugh at myself, oh, what silly fun!

The benches are waiting, for my bum to rest,
While birds hold a meeting, they're looking their best.
Each chirp is a laugh that loosens my frown,
In the echoing silence, I wear a loud crown.

When footsteps approach, the pigeons take flight,
I can't help but giggle, what a comical sight.
The world spins around, yet I'm anchored to this,
In a twist of pure laughter, I find my bliss.

Fleeting Shadows of Rhyme

A shadow danced on the wall, oh so spry,
It tripped on its toes, then waved goodbye.
The moon chuckled low, in the blanket of night,
As a cat wore a hat, oh what a silly sight!

The stars blink and giggle, like kids at play,
While the crickets sing songs, in their own funny way.
The fireflies blink as if in a race,
Creating light patterns, a whimsical space.

Each breeze tells a tale, with stumbles and slips,
While I hitch a ride on a butterfly's trips.
The night wears its laughter, a cloak all aglow,
Chasing fleeting shadows, just letting them go.

With every soft rustle, a word takes flight,
In this dance of the awkward, everything's light.
So join in the fun, there's joy to be found,
In the fleeting shadows, where humor is crowned.

Enigma of the Unsung Verse

In a world full of rhymes, the odd ones do play,
With thoughts that wander, like they've lost their way.
A squirrel wrote poetry, but forgot how to spell,
So it stuck with acorns, and that went quite well.

The clouds hold auditions, for roles up above,
While rain drops perform, in a splashy dove.
Paper boats sail, on puddle-made seas,
With dreams of big waves, oh what a tease!

Each leaf makes a joke, as it flutters down low,
While ants march in rhythm, putting on a show.
The wind is a jester, with tricks up its sleeve,
In the enigma of verses, I choose to believe.

So here's to the laughter, that spills from the trees,
And creatures around me, full of mischief and cheese.
Life's the best riddle, unfurling its quirks,
Where humor is hidden, its magic just lurks.

Tender Dreams on the Horizon

A wandering unicorn, with a fluffy white mane,
Trots through the daisies, playing the game.
Each flower it passes, it whispers a cheer,
"Life's but a journey, so grab a seat here!"

The sunbeams are tickling, they giggle and shine,
While the grass pulls a prank, and leans out of line.
A butterfly flutters, with fabulous flair,
Dressed in a costume, it's ready to dare.

While dreams softly dance, on the edge of the dusk,
A hedgehog recites, in a twist like a musk.
With giggles and grins, as the stars open wide,
Tender dreams find their place, in the joy they provide.

The night hums a tune, with a bounce in its beat,
As every small creature finds comfort, so sweet.
Tomorrow brings laughter, and fun's just a tease,
In a world of delight, I'm at perfect ease.

The Universe of Infinite Lines

In a world with no ruler, quite round,
The squiggles and jiggles jump up from the ground.
A pencil with hiccups, it scribbles away,
Chasing the clouds like a child in a play.

The stars all play tag in the inky black night,
While crayons debate on who colors it right.
A rainbow that giggles, ends not in a pot,
But spills into puddles, where dreams are all caught.

Oh, the logic is lost in this colorful spree,
Where laughter and doodles are dancing with glee.
Here wishes are jumbled, like socks in a drawer,
Each line a new punchline, who could ask for more?

So come join this circus of nonsense and flair,
Let the scribbles take flight like ducklings in air.
In the universe spun from imagination's thread,
Every silly line is a tickle to shed.

Sketching Moments Without Frame

A canvas without borders just can't be contained,
The ink starts to spill, and the laughter is gained.
With elephants waltzing and penguins in suits,
The paintbrushes gossip, debating their routes.

Here, a sun wears a hat, and the moon's a balloon,
Clouds throw confetti, and squirrels hum a tune.
Each stroke is a giggle, each color a jest,
In this party of whimsy, it's hard to contest.

Winks from a watercolor, smiles from the hue,
Every drop is a chuckle, a wink meant for you.
The portrait of chaos, so blissfully bright,
Is a sketch of the moments that tickle our sight.

So come lose yourself in this laughter-filled maze,
Where moments are memories, and silliness plays.
When framing is futile, and sketches go wild,
In this land of no limits, embrace the inner child.

Songs of the Uncontained Heart

Bouncing like bunnies, the heart beats its tune,
With rhythms of raindrops and beats from the moon.
It's a concert of chaos, a joyous cacophony,
Where giggles and grumbles create quite the symphony.

A serenade sung by a sneaky old cat,
Who's stealing the spotlight, now where is she at?
With paws tapping softly, she croons through the night,
While stars lend their voices, all twinkling with fright.

Each chorus a hiccup, each verse quite a hoot,
The joy is contagious, you can't help but scoot.
In this waltz of whimsy, where nothing's secure,
The songs of a heart can't help but endure.

So twirl in the melody, let laughter ignite,
In the dance of the unbound, where everything's right.
Let the songs be your compass, your laughter, a start,
As you skip through the symphony of your wild heart.

The Canvas of Wildest Dreams

On the canvas of dreams, the colors collide,
A splash of pure nonsense, a whimsical ride.
With penguins that tango and kittens that sing,
Each stroke is a giggle, a nonsensical fling.

A tangle of rainbows paints skies made of cake,
While marshmallows dance and the jellybeans quake.
Oh, the palette's alive with their mirth and delight,
Where worries dissolve in the glow of moonlight.

The easel is wobbly, the paints blend in glee,
As the brushes decide they're as wild as can be.
Each swirl tells a story, each dot is a laugh,
In this canvas of chaos, we sketch our own path.

So dive into madness, let creativity soar,
With laughter the anchor, let imagination explore.
For the wildest of dreams are the stitches of fun,
In this canvas of wonder, we're all just as one.

The Landscape of Lost Conventions

In a world where rhymes take naps,
And meter skips like jolly japs,
Limericks lounge on sunny shores,
As sonnets tumble through open doors.

Punctuation plays hide and seek,
While goofy verbs begin to squeak,
Adjectives dance a merry jig,
All while epic tales grow big.

Chaos reigns like cats and dogs,
As metaphors play leapfrog,
Imagery hides behind the trees,
Laughing hard at rhyming pleas.

So let conventions take a break,
And let the silly verses shake,
We'll paint the world in absurd lines,
Where laughter thrives and reason twines.

Prayers to an Unmetered Moon

Oh moon, dear moon, why are you late?
Did you stop for snacks at the silver plate?
Your rhythm's lost, your steps are swayed,
As I stumble on this unpegged parade.

With wishes thrown like frisbees wide,
I hope you join my wild ride,
But wait, your beams are all askew,
Oh silly moon, what have you brewed?

Your light is bright but lacks a beat,
Like a dancer with two left feet,
Yet here I stand with arms stretched wide,
Embracing chaos as my guide.

So I'll sing my prayers in half a tune,
To the chuckles of an unsteady moon,
May you shimmy back to the pathways true,
And twirl with glee in skies so blue.

Horizons of Untold Stories

The tales untold are dancing free,
Like squirrels tipped from a leafy spree,
Whispers trail in every breeze,
As laughter hides behind the trees.

Unwritten stories come alive,
In every nook where giggles thrive,
With characters who wear no shoes,
And welcome us to join their hues.

Here's a plot that's bound to bend,
Where time and space do not pretend,
It skips like stones on shimmering lakes,
And nudges space in wondrous flakes.

So gather 'round, let's share a plot,
Of jumbled paths and a whimsical knot,
In horizons broad where laughs impale,
And silly dreams will surely sail.

The Path Less Composed

On the path less wandered, joys abound,
With rocks that giggle and tumble around,
We'll write our thoughts on clouds floating high,
As funny rhymes leap through the sky.

Who needs a map, a strict design?
Let's chase the sun, sip on some wine,
We'll dance on letters, skip on notes,
And wear our laughter like silly coats.

Let poets frown at our free-range ways,
As we laugh louder past dreary phrases,
In a world where nonsense makes great sense,
We'll craft a journey that's most intense.

So join me, friend, on this twisted trail,
Where silly tales and giggles prevail,
In the landscape where chaos can pose,
Let's frolic down the path less composed.

The Flight of Unscripted Thoughts

A bee in a bowler hat flies by,
Whispering jokes as it drifts up high.
Pigs in top hats waltz in the breeze,
Dancing with daffodils, if you please.

Socks mismatched, a fashion delight,
Chickens wearing sunglasses, what a sight!
Clouds play checkers, high up in the blue,
The world's a stage with a cast quite askew.

A fish on a bicycle, what's going on?
Raccoons in tuxedos sing a funny song.
The sun winks, and the moon does a jig,
Life's a wild party, come dance a big dig!

Rolling in laughter, the daisies smile wide,
While turtles on roller skates take a ride.
Thoughts scatter like confetti in the air,
In this circus of whimsy, nothing is rare.

Explorations Beyond the Stanza

Octopuses playing chess in the tide,
While seahorses giggle, they cannot hide.
A llama in slippers sneezes with flair,
Tickling the planets, oh what a scare!

Squirrels in spectacles read novels aloud,
To a hippo in pajamas, all cozy and proud.
The stars drop by for a champagne toast,
To celebrate nonsense, they raise a big coast!

A rabbit in Nikes leaps over the moon,
Whispering puns while humming a tune.
Cats in pajamas play hopscotch at dusk,
Each jump creating a mystical musk.

With paper planes soaring, chaos in tow,
Each thought like a balloon, ready to go.
Let's venture beyond, it's all quite absurd,
In this world of laughter, let's fly with the bird!

Harmonies in the Untamed Air

Chickens composing symphonies so grand,
While goats strum banjos with a gentle hand.
The wind whistle-laughs, tickling my ears,
As clouds throw a party that lasts for years.

Owls in tuxedos deliver the news,
While squirrels in ties debate and amuse.
Balloons on the grass make a colorful path,
Drawing rainbows with laughter, enhancing the math.

An octopus plays drums, oh what a beat!
As fish throw confetti, quite the treat.
Jellybeans dance like they own the place,
In this carefree space, filled with funny grace.

The moon juggles stars that shimmer and twirl,
As kittens on skateboards give laughter a whirl.
A symphony of silliness, wild and free,
A concert of madness, come join the spree!

A Tapestry of Free-Flowing Ideas

Kangaroos knitting a fluffy surprise,
While gophers in bowties plan a wise guise.
A tap-dancing cactus spins around the block,
While ants in a band make a tick-tock rock.

Penguins on scooters zooming like stars,
Playing hopscotch with the moon and Mars.
The floor is a trampoline, laughter will soar,
As clowns juggle thoughts we can't help but adore.

A walrus in shades gives a winking salute,
While goldfish in bow ties don't give a hoot.
The sun makes a face, then starts to roll,
In this madcap world, it's good for the soul.

Balloons with wild dreams drift up to the sky,
As piñatas of laughter hang high and dry.
In this tapestry spun with joy and delight,
Funny thoughts wander, taking sweet flight.

www.ingramcontent.com/pod-product-compliance
Lightning Source LLC
Chambersburg PA
CBHW071820160426
43209CB00003B/149